Anne Madeliny

Neurosc

Anne Madeliny Oliveira Pereira de Sousa

Neuroscience in Teacher Training

The Contributions of Neuroscience to the Teaching and Learning Process

ScienciaScripts

Imprint

Any brand names and product names mentioned in this book are subject to trademark, brand or patent protection and are trademarks or registered trademarks of their respective holders. The use of brand names, product names, common names, trade names, product descriptions etc. even without a particular marking in this work is in no way to be construed to mean that such names may be regarded as unrestricted in respect of trademark and brand protection legislation and could thus be used by anyone.

Cover image: www.ingimage.com

This book is a translation from the original published under ISBN 978-613-9-67611-8.

Publisher:
Sciencia Scripts
is a trademark of
Dodo Books Indian Ocean Ltd. and OmniScriptum S.R.L publishing group

120 High Road, East Finchley, London, N2 9ED, United Kingdom
Str. Armeneasca 28/1, office 1, Chisinau MD-2012, Republic of Moldova, Europe

ISBN: 978-620-8-17252-7

Copyright © Anne Madeliny Oliveira Pereira de Sousa
Copyright © 2024 Dodo Books Indian Ocean Ltd. and OmniScriptum S.R.L publishing group

SUMMARY

SPECIAL THANKS 4
1 INTRODUCTION 5
CHAPTER I 12
CHAPTER II 24
REFERENCES 39
APPENDICES 43
ANNEXES 49

Anne Madeliny Oliveira Pereira de Sousa, married, mother of two children, Lucas Roberto and Anna Rebeca, aged 13 and 8. A teacher, psychopedagogue and neuropsychologist, she has loved education since 2008. When she started teaching, she was enthusiastic about contributing to her students' education, planning various actions to help them build their knowledge. However, the obstacles were numerous, there were many difficulties and barriers to the children's learning, even more so because it was a public institution, where a larger number of underprivileged children with different social problems were concentrated. Madeliny's anxiety grew every day, as she wanted to see her pupils making progress in their knowledge, but there were many learning difficulties. So she decided to seek help in scientific studies and specialized in psychopedagogy (clinical, institutional and hospital). The knowledge she acquired on the course contributed greatly to her practice, but Madeliny wanted more knowledge, so she sought to understand certain concepts in the specialization in neuropsychology. This acquired know-how opened her eyes and transformed her teaching practice.

With her experience combined with her knowledge of neuroscience, Made- liny developed projects that were satisfactory for her students and her school. She began to share her studies and research with her colleagues, and published an article on the subject. She also says that she is happy and fulfilled to be working in education, even though she knows that the difficulties are enormous and the struggle is constant for quality education. Despite the challenges, she enjoys taking part in the development of her students' knowledge and values the opportunities she has to share her experiences, thus contributing to quality education.

Address to access this CV: http://lattes.cnpq.br/0358528093172397 annemadeliny@gmail.com

I dedicate this work to my family for their support and encouragement in believing in my potential, as well as to all the education professionals who struggle with creativity and dedication to achieve our greatest goal, which is Quality Education for All.

SPECIAL THANKS

First of all to God, for being with me at all times, being my refuge and strength on difficult days. In addition to giving me the privilege of sharing experiences during the course of this work, and for enabling me to experience yet another victory. My eternal gratitude goes to him. To my dear mother Taiza Maria for her encouragement and support. And especially to my husband Màbio Roberto A. de Sousa and my children Lucas Roberto and Anna Rebeca for helping me to carry out this project and for understanding my absence at many times.

1 INTRODUCTION

The challenges and demands faced by education in contemporary society, together with technological advances, make knowledge a strategic issue for economic, political and social progress. Thus, there is a need to critically rethink the social function of education and the changes in a globalized society. Faced with these facts, education is being questioned about the need for a culture that aims to create a real learning environment that is conducive to these changes. The complexity of teaching and learning is the main challenge facing education today. Considering that the educator has the objective of promoting the formation of critical and reflective citizens, awakening the necessary artifices to deal with the references accessible in modern society, leading to the structuring of knowledge. For this to actually happen, an up-to-date and democratic education system is needed, taking on the responsibility and commitment of building a concrete learning landscape that meets the demands of modern society. However, it is essential to define objectives, strategic goals and the action plan that such a system must have in order to achieve them. Ensuring the development of each student's intellectual potential is an important factor in attesting to the development of the skills and competencies needed for them to act in society.

The bill, approved in 2010, articulates the National Education Plan (PNE - 2011/2020 -PL n° 8.035/2010), presenting ten objective guidelines and 20 goals. One of these, number 15.7, aims to "Promote curricular reform of undergraduate courses in order to ensure a focus on student learning, dividing the workload into general training, training in the area of knowledge and specific didactics" (PNE - 2011/2020, p. 44).

The mission to be developed by the teacher requires clarity, and it is necessary to have defined goals and objectives, to be aware of what to teach, for whom to teach, and it is in this vision that the how to develop permeates. Bearing in mind the integration of various aspects of the teaching-learning process, taking into account the student as a whole, knowledge, teaching strategies and the cultural and historical context in which they find themselves (cf. TACCA, 2000).

From this point of view, scientific studies on the central nervous system, which is currently undergoing great development, can help to broaden theoretical concepts in teacher training, leading to an understanding of the complexity of the teaching-learning process. Neuroscience is a science that studies the chemical, structural and functional development of the nervous system.

This science is present in different fields of knowledge, contributing directly to scientific progress in various areas, such as medicine, psychology, linguistics and philosophy, becoming, in recent years, one of the educational sciences. In education, Neuroscience seeks to understand how the brain behaves in the learning process and how it learns (cf. COSENZA; GUERRA, 2011).

As a result of neuroscientist convictions and their discoveries regarding human cognitive development, teacher training must undergo a period of reinvention and updating. According to GADOTTI (2008), for there to be quality education, teacher qualification is a strategic point. However, it is complex to properly structure the parameters for this qualification, considering that teacher training courses with their content and methodologies are outdated or, at the very least, "static" - because they are based on an instructional view (unilateralized by traditional methods) of teaching. This is why there is a need to rethink changes to the teacher training process. In this way, educators can be legitimized for more meaningful, efficient and autonomous actions. Knowing that they are the protagonists in the neurobiological transformations that build learning, but have no knowledge of how the brain works.

For this reason, educational management is fundamental, both for organizing institutions and for mobilizing professionals to improve the quality of teaching. Throughout the history of educational management in Brazil, great efforts have been made to improve the quality of education, but most of them represent isolated actions that only mitigate the situation. Even if there are tools that help bring about this improvement, they are ineffective due to the lack of articulated and joint actions that act on a macro-structural scenario. In this sense, to think about educational management is to understand its meaning as a conscious articulation between the activities that take place in the daily life of the school institution and their social and political significance (cf. LUCK, 1999).

In recent years, the state of Ceará has been advancing in public policies that value pedagogical intervention, understanding that actions to qualify teachers are necessary for the effective development of its citizens in training, understanding that leading a classroom requires essential skills that cannot be ignored. Being a teacher requires *knowing, knowing how to do and*, above all, *knowing how to be*. The competitiveness of the modern world, the new technologies that occur in short spaces of time, generate the search for continuous and satisfactory learning. In this way, the state of Ceará implemented the Literacy at an Early Age Program.

Certa (PAIC)[1] which has been motivating the municipalities of Ceará to seek out new concepts that are fundamental to pedagogical knowledge, providing theoretical subsidies for teaching action.

In this fight for quality education, the state of Ceará has been developing a satisfactory participatory democratic management approach, recognizing the need to make all students literate in the early years of elementary school, as well as making municipal managers responsible for the quality of education, in addition to applying external evaluations that make it possible to plan innovative pedagogical interventions. The PAIC has shown excellent results[2] , leading Brazil to embrace its program and turn it into a National Pact.[3] The municipality of Quixadà joined the National Pact for Literacy at the Right Age (PNAIC) - of which I have been a study advisor since 2013 -, a formal agreement embraced by the federal, state and municipal governments to ensure that all children are literate by the age of eight, at the end of the 3rd year of elementary school.

In 2013, the team of PNAIC advisors of which I am a member carried out a series of visits to the Regional Education Offices. During this monitoring, we had the opportunity to take a closer look at the factors that were favorable indicators for the

---

1 For more information on the PAIC, see http://www.paic.seduc.ce.gov.br/.
2 The results of the program can be accessed at:
http://www.paic.seduc.ce.gov.br/index.php/resultados/mapas-dos-resultados.
3 More information at: http://pacto.mec.gov.br/index.php.

development of quality in education, as well as the negative practices that needed to be reframed. Taking into account the factors presented in the situational results of the monitoring of the schools by the technical team of the Municipal Education Department, it became necessary to build a plan of actions that could promote the learning of the students assisted in the schools, as well as strengthening the democratic and participatory management of the school community.

Based on the concept of *quality management*, we can report that the Municipal Department of Education in which we work develops actions that reflect participatory management and that the educational plan aims to develop ideas associated with meaningful and interdisciplinary teaching, seeking quality in the educational process, with the main objective being the critical and participatory formation of the citizen. This action plan includes the ongoing training of educators, in which we develop our actions to integrate the concepts of neuroscience with the teaching and learning process. According to Morales (2005, p. 10): "mental states come from patterns of neural activity, so learning is achieved through the stimulation of neural connections, which can be strengthened depending on the quality of the pedagogical intervention" - by having this knowledge the teachers participating in our training have already reported changes in their teaching practice.

It is necessary to propose a transformative education in which the acquisition of knowledge takes place through the transformation of the previous knowledge that the student brings to school into scientific knowledge. Making the teaching process a constant action-reflection-action, where the teacher researches, experiments, discusses with other educators, concludes and resumes the course of the process, considering learning as the main objective. For this to happen, the educator has to be enthusiastic, believe in their students, have a friendly relationship in search of new knowledge that will give meaning to their students' lives.

For Vygotsky, social experiences are involved in higher mental processes of adaptive self-regulation. In this view, the primary purpose of educational institutions is to help develop the student's ability to concentrate, reason and learn (cf. RELVAS, 2003).

In reality, we must understand that the right to education starts from the recognition that systematic knowledge is significant for the intellectual development of the subject. However, in order to have a quality education, we need professionals with solid pedagogical and scientific training, who are open to change, because assimilating the functioning of the brain allows for a better understanding of learning and consequently the improvement of didactics.

Based on the above and the recognition of the inferences related to the functioning of the brain in the process of acquiring learning, which are still not appreciated in many teacher training courses, we highlight the relevance of developing studies that contribute to the training of education professionals in this knowledge, because if modern society is constantly changing and education is part of this same society, we wonder how teachers are coping with the need for this new knowledge to improve their teaching: Are teachers aware that their pedagogical practice triggers neurological and hormonal reactions in the student's body that can influence their motivation to learn? In this sense, the proposal to unite Neuroscience and Education in teacher training aims to collaborate in a participatory way in an efficient and effective training for teachers in the basic education system.

In view of the concepts presented, we understand the relevance of teachers' knowledge of the methods involved in the acquisition of learning in the brain, since such knowledge can provide differentiated strategies and effective methods for learning. The need to ensure the right to education for all has to be seen and understood by educational managers from the perspective of guaranteeing learning, with the aim of encouraging our educators to build and develop new curricula in an autonomous, collective and creative way, so that they can develop actions that provide formative experiences, making everyday school life a space for reflection and the construction of knowledge.

In view of this, this research aims to integrate the concept of Neuroscience into the training of teachers of the National Pact for Literacy at the Right Age (PNAIC) in the education system of the municipality of Quixadà in the state of Ceará, in order to present the importance of knowledge on this subject for changes in pedagogical methodology, in addition to intensifying the theoretical foundation presented in the study notebooks[4] contributing to teaching practice, as well as strengthening and conducting the teaching-learning process.

The study project in question was carried out through a qualitative approach, using semi-structured interviews, as well as a review of scientific literature in articles and books to organize concepts and theoretical references. The research work will enable moments of study based on neuroscience in the training of thirty literacy teachers from the 2nd year of elementary school who are taking part in PNAIC in the municipality of Quixadà, the city where I work as Pedagogical Coordinator at the Municipal Department of Education and study advisor for the Pact. The content covered in the training will be associated with neuroscientific concepts, and the teachers will be encouraged to apply the theory to practice, and their validity will be verified through questionnaires, *on-site* observation and data analysis with teaching monitoring tools, as well as the use of media resources.

In this way, the study will seek to verify the interference of the understanding of Neuroscience in the training of educators in the basic education system and the need to take into account the knowledge produced by neuroscience research when planning, articulating and developing their didactic projects. For the acquisition of learning, there are some common concepts that can be adjusted for everyone, but there are situations that are specific, originating from the social context of each one, so the educator must know in order to be able to analyze or treat in a differentiated way. We know that we won't be able to break with an old tradition focused on assessing and teaching in a single, standardized way overnight.

The work will be divided into two chapters, both with subdivisions. In the first chapter, we will present an analysis of the neuroscientific contribution to academic training in pedagogy courses at public universities in the state of Ceará and in the National Network for Continuing Teacher Training, as well as a study of the applicability of

---

[4]More information at: http://pacto.mec.gov.br/2012-09-19-19-09-11.

neuroscience in education. In its subdivision, we will comment on the relevance of knowledge of Neuroscience for the training of educators. In chapter two, we will report on the integration of neuroscientific knowledge in PNAIC teacher training in the municipality of Quixadà, exploring theory in practice, as well as some successful experiences. At the end of this project, we will present possible results, as well as making available in the form of annexes the instruments and photos of the study.

CHAPTER I

1 . NEUROSCIENCE IN EDUCATION.

To begin this research, we conducted a search to find out the curricula of the pedagogy courses at the public universities in the state of Ceará - it should be noted that the investigation was limited to public institutions because they are the main partners in permanent training, including the one in which we carried out this study. Let's look at the institutions: 1) UFC[5] - Universidade Federal do Ceará, 2) UECE[6] - Universidade Estadual do Ceará, 3) UVA[7] - Universidade Estadual Vale do Acaraù and 4) URCA[8] - Universidade Regional do Cariri, with the aim of verifying the existence of subjects that included the study of neuroscience. However, none of these universities had any. This aroused even more interest in researching the contribution of neuroscience to education. In this way, we focused on the National Network for Continuing Teacher Training[9], which was created in 2004 to help improve teacher and student training, with a priority on educators in the basic education network of the public education system. The fields covered for training were: literacy and language, mathematics and science education, humanities and social sciences teaching, arts and physical education.

The Ministry of Education provides technical and financial support and is responsible for managing the development of the program, which the states, municipalities and the Federal District join on a collaborative basis. Among the teacher training courses we can mention, for example:

Pró-Letramento: which seeks to create an organization that works in an integrated way, aiming to improve learning in the initial years of elementary school, with the following objectives: 1) offering support to teachers' pedagogical practice, helping to boost the quality of teaching and learning in Portuguese language and mathematics; 2)

---

[5] http://www.si3.ufc.br/sigaa/public/curso/curriculo.j sf;j sessionid=E6546E4B8981AD11C01C5CA112 E3A0D3.node147 Searched on 08/08/2014.
[6] http://www.uece.br/uece/index.php/graduacao/presenciais - searched on 30/07/2014.
[7] http://www.uvanet.br/ - search on 30/07/2014
[8] It was not possible to access the curriculum as it was not available on the institution's website.
[9] http://pacto.mec.gov.br/component/content/article/26-eixos-de-atuacao/54-formacao

suggesting situations that motivate the construction and reflection of knowledge as a continuous process of teacher training; as well as 3) adding new knowledge that makes it possible to understand mathematics and language and their teaching and learning processes.

Proinfo: which refers to an integrated training program aimed at the didactic-pedagogical use of Information and Communication Technologies - ICT in everyday school life, linked to the delivery of technological supplies to schools and the supply of content, multimedia and digital resources offered by the Teacher's Portal;

Training in the National Pact for Literacy at the Right Age: aimed at literacy teachers, proposing study methodology and practical activities.

These courses present methodology and theoretical foundations that value the construction of knowledge and the subject as the protagonist of learning, as well as considering the educator as the mediator of this process. When analyzing their content, we see that pedagogical practice is valued alongside the theoretical basis, giving importance to the basic mental schemes and processes for the development of learning. However, it does not explicitly present the need to know how learning takes place in the brain and how this knowledge can help teaching practice.

In view of these analyses, the question arises as to the real importance of teachers' knowledge of scientific advances and their contribution to planning and articulating lessons aimed at meaningful learning. Various studies have proven the support of neuroscience in the teaching-learning process.

The Quixadà municipal education system is divided into sixteen educational regions, subdivided into levels that characterize the number of schools and the managers responsible for running them. Quixadà has been participating in the Literacy at the Right Age Program since 2007, with significant advances and setbacks, which are analyzed in order to understand the reasons why progress has been discontinued.

This analysis shows the need to intensify the credibility of some education professionals, as well as pedagogical support for the applicability of training in the classroom, since the regions that made progress were made up of managers who were familiar with the programs being implemented in the municipality, whether at state or national level, developing integrated work. Pedagogical directors took part in teacher planning, encouraging ongoing training and contributing to the implementation of actions in the school.

From this reflection arose the need to plan actions with the literacy teachers of PNAIC, integrating subjects of scientific knowledge with teacher training, seeking to contribute to the quality of education. In 2013, the municipality of Quixadà signed up to the PNAIC, with 142 teachers and 6 study guides. I was one of the study guides and developed these actions in the 3rd grade classes, with 23 teachers, but the project was not actually drawn up, it was only in 2014 that the research was organized in an organized way. Quixadà currently has 791 students in the literacy cycle in the 1st year, 812 students in the 2nd year and 984 students in the 3rd year, the number of teachers is 55 in the 1st year, 57 in the 2nd year and 64 in the 3rd year, we have 06 study advisors, however, only 30 literacy teachers in the 2nd year are part of this project, as they are the ones who took part in my training. Of these teachers, 4 took part in my training in 2013.

PNAIC was born out of the need to guarantee the right to full learning at the end of the literacy cycle. We have a cruel reality in Brazilian history of children finishing school without being literate. This Pact is made up of an integrated set of actions, materials[10], curricular and pedagogical references to be made available by the Ministry of Education - MEC.

The main thrust of the PNAIC is the continued training of literacy teachers, contributing to their professional improvement, as well as proposing the construction of proposals to define the learning and development rights of children in the first three years of elementary school. The face-to-face course lasts 120 hours per year and is based on the Pro-Literacy Program, whose methodology proposes studies and practical actions. The training sessions with the literacy teachers are carried out by Study

---

10 Teaching materials, literary works, teaching aids, games and educational technologies.

Advisors.

Study guides take part in a specific course, lasting 200 hours a year, run by public universities. The set of study books[11] for teacher training is intended to support discussions related to face-to-face continuing training, with the aim of deepening the debate on literacy from the perspective of literacy.

The training provides methodological guidelines for the development of Learning Rights within the literacy cycle. The didactic work developed in these studies prioritizes reflection-action-reflection, putting theory into practice. The universalization of practice can be applied based on an understanding of two factors: the content explored in the classroom and the methodology, dynamics and procedures for presenting the content. It is of fundamental importance to value the student as the protagonist of learning, respecting their way of thinking and their logic in the process of constructing knowledge.

At the start of the PNAIC training courses in 2014, a questionnaire was administered to check teachers' prior knowledge of neuroscience. The results can be seen in the following graphs:

---

11 http://pacto.mec.gov.br/2012-09-19-19-09-11.

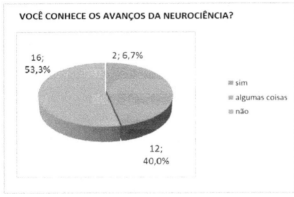

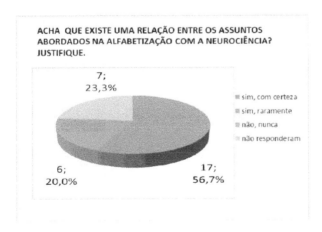

Among the reasons given are the following:

- As neuroscience studies the mind, this will certainly help in the literacy process.
- It is in literacy that we discover something new, organize our brains and appropriate meaningful knowledge.
- I don't know anything about neuroscience yet, so it's difficult to answer.
- I can't answer that.

AO ELABORAR ATIVIDADES PARA SEUS ALUNOS LEVA EM CONSIDERÇÃO O MODO DE APRENDIZAGEM DO CEREBRO? POR QUÊ?

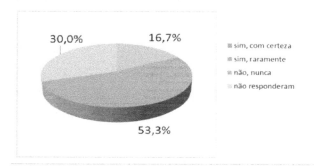

Among the reasons given are the following:

- Because many children may not be suitable for a particular subject.
- Yes, because the brain is present in all human activities.
- Because learning happens according to the maturation of the brain.
- This is because the activities designed help to retain what has been learned.

COSTUMA UTILIZAR ATIVIDADES LÚDICAS PARA REFORÇAR O CONTEÚDO LEVANDO EM CONSIDERAÇÃO O FUNCIONAMENTO DO CÉREBRO? JUSTIFIQUE.

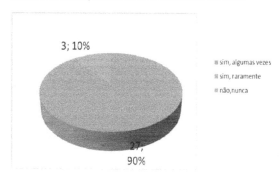

Among the reasons given are the following:

- Yes, it's with play in our classes that we get the most students, because that way they learn through play.

- In the literacy process, play is necessary, but I hadn't thought about how the brain works.

- I believe that playfulness favors learning, facilitates the development of understanding.

- Yes, but I wasn't thinking about how the brain works.

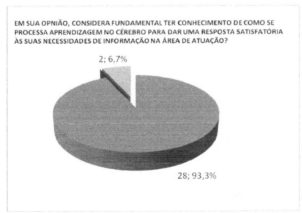

Among the reasons given are the following:

- For work to be successful, we need to acquire knowledge in order to develop skills.
- Yes, because it will improve my classroom practice.
- If we don't have this knowledge, we won't know how to act.
- By understanding the brain's learning process, we can devise effective strategies.

Among the suggestions asked for in the questionnaire we can highlight the following:

• That they bring us knowledge that contributes to our practice.

- Bring in more in-depth neuroscience studies.
- Let's have lectures and moments of study on the subject.
- Improving new knowledge based on PNAIC.

An analysis of these graphs showed the importance of linking relevant neuroscience issues to the content contained in the PNAIC training study books. The pact's teaching materials also include booklets on inclusive education and rural education, which should cover all the topics to be studied. Thus began the journey to choose scientific knowledge that most closely related to the themes being worked on in the training courses. Below is a table of the scientific subjects and content explored in the meetings:

PNAIC - 2013	PNAIC - 2014	NEURO SCIENCE
Curriculum in the Literacy Cycle;	Organization of pedagogical work;	Concept and relationship between neuroscience and education;
Planning and Organizing the Routine in Literacy;	Quantification, records and groupings;	How the brain works - (learning - stimulation from the environment - new synapses between neurons);
Appropriation of the Alphabetic Writing System and the Consolidation of the Literacy Process;	Problem-solving operations;	Learning and memory; Video: recipe for learning better and faster - intelligent repetition;
Playfulness;	Building the decimal numbering system;	Principles of neuroscience as a potential application in the classroom environment;
Working with Textual Genres;	Geometry;	Meaningful learning; Video: neuroscience and learning;
Teaching Projects and Teaching Sequences with the different curricular components;	Statistical education;	Evolution of knowledge, learning strategies;
Heterogeneity in the Classroom and Learning Rights;	Mathematical knowledge and other fields of knowledge;	Neuroscience x Education - a two-way street; video: Series - Brain, learning machine 01.
School Progression and	Games in mathematical	Investigating the basis of learning through

Assessment;	literacy;	neuroscience can contribute to quality education;
Seminar.	Seminar.	Exchange of experiences and presentation of successful lessons.

The training sessions are held once a month, with 12 hours in person and 4 hours of extra activities - such as visits to other institutions to exchange experiences, planning and other actions. The study advisors fill their hours with pedagogical support. In its action plan, the Municipal Secretary of Education has scheduled visits to the Regional Education Offices at least twice a month, so that we can monitor the applicability of the guidelines given in the training courses with regard to planning as well as teaching methodology in the classroom, with the aim of contributing to the success of our students.

During these visits, the actions are observed and recorded on instruments, so that at the end of the visit the observations are shared and the necessary referrals are made to the teachers and managers. In the same way, meetings are held with the technicians from the Education Department who monitor each Regional Education Office, in an attempt to build participatory management.

At the beginning of the visits, we noticed some relevant points in relation to the teaching practice of the research participants, which we need to observe, as well as changes in the same relevant points after the fifth training course. See the table below:

	Relevant points	Yes	No	In part	After 5th formation Yes	No	In part
1. interaction between the students and the content	- Are the activities and problems proposed challenging and useful for all students or was it too easy for some and too difficult for others?	07	04	19	-	07	-	23
	- Há the resumption of Knowledge worked on in previous lessons as a starting point to facilitate new learning or do the activities just put into play what is already known by the class?	04	11	15	-	09	06	15
	- Does the teacher select and organize the content in a way that promotes meaningful learning for the students?	13	04	13	-	16	-	17

	Relevant points	Yes	No	In part	After 5th formation	Yes	No	In part
	- Do the students participate in class, actively interacting in the proposed activities?	10	02	18	-	16	02	11
2. The teacher's pedagogical stance	Relevant points	Yes	No	In part	After 5th formation	Yes	No	In part
	- Does the teacher use targeted techniques/strategies in ongoing training?	13	08	09	-	17	3	10
	- Does the teacher use a methodology that involves all the students?	07	06	17	-	11	03	16
3. Lesson preparation and planning	Relevant points	Yes	No	In part	After 5th formation	Yes	No	In part
	- Do the students' progress and difficulties perceived by the teacher promote the "replanning" of didactic-pedagogical actions?	13	08	09	-	17	03	16
4. Material used	Relevant points	Yes	No	In part	After 5th formation	Yes	No	In part
	- Does the teacher use different materials?	14	08	08	-	17	03	10
	- Is the amount of material used sufficient for teaching practice?	13	-	17	-	16	-	14
5. Presentation of content	Relevant points	Yes	No	In part	After 5th formation	Yes	No	In part
	- Is the concentration of the students during the exposition of the contents?	09	08	13	-	13	07	10
	- Do you use moderate gestures that match your speech?	11	04	15	-	15	04	11
	- Use your voice properly.	11	04	15	-	15	04	11

The face-to-face meetings are structured as follows: presentation of the objectives of the workbook in question, associated with the chosen subject of neuroscience. Reading the memory of the previous training, recalling what was worked on in the previous training. Exploring the content through *slides*, videos, dynamics, moments of group study, exchanging experiences, presenting work and showing successful lessons, as well as preparing didactic projects with didactic sequences and making games related to learning rights.

It is understood that sensory information reaches the brain through nerve connections that are accelerated and dynamic. This is due to the integration of three essential systems for the acquisition of knowledge by the learner. The first element is the information system, the second is the understanding of the biological system and the third refers to cybernetics, which is linked to our daily lives, thus building a web of connectivity.

By knowing how the central nervous system works, teachers can articulate their pedagogical practice, reflecting on the development of mental schemes and the evolution of students. This way, they can intervene in various learning difficulties, seeking to alleviate or remedy possible impediments in the teaching and learning process. Understanding that the concepts acquired by neuroscience can contribute to the rise of education, aiming for quality and favorable results for its students.

2.1 - THE IMPORTANCE OF KNOWLEDGE OF NEUROSCIENCE FOR THE TRAINING OF EDUCATORS

Studies are being carried out to analyze the relevance of neuroscience in education. Neuroscientists, psychologists and pedagogues are analyzing whether this knowledge is an important element to help in the current situation of teaching and learning, because neuroscience applied to education is not aimed at a new scientific theory of education, but at a scientific understanding of education.

Cosenza reports on his practical experience running courses on aspects of neuroscience connected to learning processes and education:

> Educators, teachers and parents, as well as psychologists, neurologists and psychiatrists are, in a way, the people who work most with the brain. Rather than intervening when it doesn't work properly, educators contribute to the organization of the learner's nervous system and, therefore, the behaviours they will display throughout their lives. And this is a task of great responsibility! It is therefore curious that they do not know how the brain works (COSENZA, 2011, p. 7).

We understand the need for teachers to seek knowledge about brain function and stimulate its connections, understanding that the brain changes with each new experience, improving reasoning and memory capacity. Therefore, plasticity is the brain's ability to alter the functioning of the perceptual and motor system based on transformations in the environment. As such, the brain has no limits, it never loses its ability to change. Therefore, by enabling other brain connections, using different methodologies, exploring previous knowledge and determining relationships between new content, the educator will be contributing to satisfactory learning and building solid memories.

Morris and Fillenz (2003) comment that emotional state can influence the efficiency of learning, since we are more inclined to remember facts associated with pleasant, distressing or unhappy experiences. We also recall facts more carefully when we are attentive. The central nervous system shows neuronal plasticity (*synaptogenesis*), but broad synaptic consistency does not establish a better ability to learn. Students need to feel involved in the actions and co-responsible for school activities, understanding that the subjects worked on are essential for their lives.

It is necessary to rethink the actions directed by the educator in the teaching and learning process, because the act of studying needs to be planned. Learning takes place through the development of organized ideas. When educators guide, suggest, remind and praise, they are contributing to the structuring of knowledge. Intelligence doesn't come from accumulating content, but from organizing it.

It should be emphasized that the teacher is the stimulator in the construction of knowledge, leading the student to experience everyday actions in problem solving, analyzing and suggesting hypotheses, enabling them to take a leading role in the directed tasks. And thus ensure meaningful learning. We know the importance of questioning when carrying out the activities proposed to the student, encouraging them to reflect on actions and to develop the process of internalizing the content learned. In this process, students retrieve their previous knowledge and integrate it with new information, thus reorganizing their learning into new scientific concepts. Neuroscientific knowledge can effectively influence the construction of learning. Neuronal circuits can be strengthened through teaching practices.

CHAPTER II

3 - APPLICABILITY OF NEUROSCIENCE IN TEACHER TRAINING FROM PNAIC IN THE MUNICIPALITY OF QUIXADA

The main objective of the Quixadà Municipal Education Department is to develop educational policies that ensure and implement actions aimed at the quality of education, focusing on teaching and learning processes. In the action plan of the Pedagogical Development Superintendence, of which I am a member, being responsible for the Pedagogical Development Coordination for Elementary School I, it is planned to promote ongoing training for teachers, with the aim of improving teaching action in order to optimize the learning process, encouraging effective participation by teachers in the meetings, as well as indicating bibliographical references contributing to their ongoing training.

Based on this educational policy, the *Neuroscience in Teacher Training* project was created to strengthen teaching management through actions that seek to improve effective classroom practices. The literacy teachers who are part of this research in the municipality of Quixadà received a proposal in their first training course to develop differentiated training courses, where we would explore neuroscience knowledge associated with the content we were to study. Everyone liked the proposal and so a semi-open training schedule was presented, containing some subjects we could study and asking for suggestions. In the course of the debate, we agreed on some subjects that were considered essential for teacher development.

The most talked-about topic is related to the guiding principles of neuroscience for education, so together we built the final training schedule, understanding what is portrayed in the work of Cosenza and Guerra (2011). According to these authors, making use of different channels of access to the central nervous system and information processing makes a difference, and the process of elaboration, repetition and consolidation must be respected, so that teaching strategies are more likely to be successful, as they will be taking into account the brain's way of learning.

The integration of the neuroscientist community with teachers needs to be a two-way street, taking part in the conflicts generated in the school community. In order to develop research and studies that can analyze the positive or negative consequences of certain pedagogical interventions in relation to neural functioning. Strategies were then planned based on integrating the content covered in the PNAIC study books with neuroscientific knowledge, intensifying understanding of the topics covered and combating resistance to application on the part of certain educators who make up the municipal education network because they don't believe in its effects.

Over the course of the training sessions, we developed several welcoming dynamics that explored socialization and building bonds. These activities could be adapted for the students, such as the balloon dynamic, which explored the shared reading of fragmented texts that were inside the balloons after the game of popping a colleague's balloon. As well as the change dynamic, the teachers would stand in pairs, one in front of the other, watching their colleague for a few seconds. As a study guide, I would report the commands, where first we would ask them to turn around and without the other realizing it, develop an action that would modify their characteristics at that moment, so that when the command was given back, the colleague would discover what had been modified, each round increasing the number of actions that had to be modified and consequently changing the degree of difficulty. This dynamic developed moments of reflection about the difficulties that human beings have in modifying actions from old cultures, in the face of new conceptions that often require a special look and acceptability so that everything that is learned is actually practiced.

Brain plasticity requires environmental stimuli and life experiences. These interventions influence neural plasticity and learning, with plastic changes being the way in which we learn (cf. ROTTA, 2006).

The way we think is determined by essential factors in the social context in which the learner develops through their own history. Human cognitive abilities and ways of structuring thought are the result of actions carried out in accordance with the social customs of the culture in which the subject develops (cf. VYGOTSKY, 2000).

In the studies covered, we present *slides of* the unit's objectives, exploring the understanding of the subject to be worked on and deepening knowledge through dynamics, videos, debates, group studies and interdisciplinary space with other areas of knowledge, as well as presentations of work and exchange of successful experiences of activities developed in the classroom.

The meetings have made it possible to learn a great deal, for example: in the theme on *playfulness*, entitled "Let's play at reinventing stories", which took place after some training sessions in 2013, it was possible to apply the knowledge learned so far and analyze the acquisition of knowledge in other areas that influence the learning process. In this action, the teachers were motivated and the level of acceptance had increased among those who didn't believe in the program. We noticed that, as they acquired new knowledge, they were already participating enthusiastically.

At the beginning of the training, we welcomed the participants with a good morning video and a spontaneous prayer. We explored memory reading, reflecting on the content covered, reviewing the theme "Appropriation of the Alphabetic Writing System and the Consolidation of the Literacy Process", associating learning and memory, which in the previous training was the subject discussed in the space reserved for interdisciplinarity with another area of knowledge (neuroscience), as well as recalling the video lesson "Recipe for learning better and faster: intelligent repetition!". The theme portrayed the importance of the educator getting the student to think about the subject, developing activities that will activate various brain connections.

The individual's interactions with the environment lead to synaptic transformations and the appearance of new synapses by intensifying neural connections with useful activities. On the other hand, synaptic connections that are little used become weaker or disappear. The selection of connections that will be conserved and strengthened depends on the stimuli the brain receives. Learning, memory, cognition and teaching are related and confer on the essential activities that take place in the school institution (cf. MORRIS; FILLENZ, 2003). This is confirmed by Cosenza & Guerra:

The modern world is very different from the one in which our brains evolved. Today, there isn't always an adequately structured environment for the development of executive functions. This is a problem that should be taken into account if we really want to educate our young people for a useful and happy life. (COSENZA; GUERRA, 2011, p. 98)

We know that the brain system is willing to learn what it understands to be significant. Therefore, it is necessary to be selective with the information we intend to process, analyzing its relevance, understanding that short-term memory will not always be able to process everything that is required of it. On some occasions, it is necessary to limit the stimuli and benefit from the information that needs to be learned.

In order to intensify understanding of the importance of developing actions learned in PNAIC, *slides* were presented with the objectives of the unit, exploring the understanding of the subject worked on: the importance of play, associated with the principles of neuroscience as a potential application in the classroom environment, leading us to reflect on Assmann's (2001) conception, which aims to pass on to education the understanding of learning as a structural junction, implying a new conception of learning, which is based on the fact that learning experiences in pedagogical contexts give rise to changes in the subject's structure. Experiences in the classroom provoke significant reflections on thoughts, feelings and actions, allowing learning to be acquired as a reconstructive process, involving the mental and emotional self-organization of those connected in this context.

During this training, we played a game of reinventing the story "Little Red Riding Hood". We created a large circle where we would start the storytelling, and two teachers would hold signs with various words, which they would introduce into the context of the retelling as they were presented, observing their coherence. This was a lively and satisfying moment, as we delved deeper into the topic and the construction of a new story took place.

According to Posner and Raichle (2001), cognitive systems are linked to the mental operations that carry out everyday human activities - such as reading, writing, talking and planning. The cognitive system of language, for example, involves speaking, reading and writing, activating different brain structures. In the view of Moraes (2004), learning progresses through dynamic movements of exchange, analysis and increasingly complex self-regulating synthesis, going beyond the volume of information and being remade, through transformation, by means of structural changes arising from actions and interactions.

Memory is responsible for storing information, as well as for searching for what is stored. Learning requires skills to deal in an organized way with new information, or with information already stored in the brain, in order to carry out new actions (cf. POSNER; RAICHLE, 2001).

In 2014, the training sessions were full of new things, as PNAIC introduced the importance of linking mathematics to language, showing the need for children to produce their own teaching materials and play games.

Training sessions were therefore planned using games, exploring their objectives, associating them with learning rights and assessment descriptors.

In the meetings we worked on the construction of the decimal numbering system and geometry, which were associated with neuroscientific issues that portray meaningful learning and the principles of neuroscience as a potential application in the classroom environment, these trainings were considered the best so far, in which we used *slide* studies and neuroimaging exams. Neuroimaging technology has shown surprising results in interpreting anatomy as well as the functioning of the human brain. These advances encourage the search for the results of its application in education, in understanding how the brain learns, determining a new paradigm in educational practices. Understanding how human beings learn is essential for educators, as it is an essential subject for their initial and continuing academic training, as it enables them to play a key role in education. Much is questioned about how people learn, but little about how they are taught.

For this reason, the games used in these meetings were: "golden bank", aimed at understanding the characteristics of the decimal system, from groupings of 10 in 10, we developed regrouping and exchanges; the "dominoes game", which explored spatial awareness and the operations of addition and subtraction, they had to fit the pieces on the board so that the lateralities gave the same quantities determined by the conductor of the rules; the "tangram", a puzzle made up of seven pieces with well-known geometric shapes, these pieces allow several ways to compose figures. This last game can be developed to achieve different objectives, such as: composing and decomposing figures; identifying geometric shapes; relating elements of a figure; illustrating stories, among other things. The challenge was to start playing, always using seven pieces for each figure, initially forming only flat figures and not overlapping the pieces and presenting the figure through a textual genre, with the aim of developing communication.

Another game is the "password game", which has the following rules: the study leader, who is the challenger, hides some words and proposes that the other person finds them. The participants make their moves by receiving information from the challenger corresponding to the secret words. The game ends when the participant's answer matches what the challenger has hidden. This activity has implications such as: it stimulates deduction and inference; it works on the construction and verification of hypotheses; it resembles the interpretation of a text and enables cooperation.

In the first two games, we worked on logical reasoning and mental calculation (adding and taking away). In addition to these activities, a number of dynamics were applied, including the construction of a story using a bank of words from a text chosen by the study supervisor on the history of geometry. Unbeknownst to the teachers, these words had to be included in the context of the type and genre of text that the teachers had selected; the aim of this activity was to get the teachers to associate mathematical concepts with language.

According to Vygotsky (2000), a concept can only be realized when the subject's own mental development has reached the necessary level. Knowing that, a concept is a legitimate and complex act of thinking, which cannot be taught through incessant repetition alone.

It is understood to be something beyond certain associative links made by memory; it is more than a simple mental practice. The expansion of concepts requires the development of many cognitive functions: coherent memory, abstraction, the ability to equate and distinguish, among others. These complex mental processes cannot be directed by initial learning alone. It is unlikely that concepts can be taught directly, a fact confirmed by practical experience.

The trainings are also developed with presentations of various videos that have intensified the relationship between neuroscience and education with extra classroom activities, always aimed at the elaboration of projects or lesson plans with didactic objectives, associating learning rights with their applicability recorded in photos or murals, favoring the exchange of experiences. It is important to understand how teaching can lead to the development of intellectual skills, through the formation of concepts and the development of theoretical reasoning, as well as the resources through which students can improve and strengthen their learning.

In order to guarantee efficient learning, it is necessary to have a pedagogical practice that takes brain function into account, motivating the learner's involvement with the teacher and the content (cf. ALVAREZ, 2006).

3.1 - SUCCESSFUL EXPERIENCES.

Teacher training gives rise to a variety of studies and reflections, seeking answers on how to develop teaching in a differentiated, qualitative and learner-oriented way. Throughout the training, we built up new knowledge based on the PNAIC study books with some provocations linked to neuroscience, such as: What is the purpose of memory in the learning process? Why do we remember some things and forget others? Which of the senses interferes more in the acquisition of learning? Can we learn several things at the same time? Does everyone learn in the same way or differently? We use these reflections to work out strategies for dealing with the situations we encounter in everyday life in the classroom, such as lack of attention, difficulties in the teaching and learning process, poor assimilation, lack of understanding, among other anxieties.

During the training sessions, we were able to understand what is important to be assimilated in different ways, using different languages, images, humor, art, drawing, practicing storytelling to create the necessary conditions for our students to learn.

According to Philippe Perrenoud (2001), there shouldn't just be a list of competencies, there needs to be a broader dimension, so that educators aren't just technicians. In other words, what would be interesting would be a dimension that is capable of reflection, of learning incessantly from experience, transforming and building knowledge in the course of the professional journey.

In the extra activities, we guided the production of interdisciplinary didactic projects with various curricular components, taking into account the social context of each student, as well as didactic sequences with clear objectives, with individual monitoring of the skills developed in the learning process, filling out instruments that helped in the interventions. We know that this process is not easy, but these activities were developed in a satisfactory way, and we were honored with presentations of these actions in the training sessions, as well as having the pleasure of following their process in the classroom. Progress was made through the exchange of experiences and the acquisition of new knowledge, which led to successful lessons and progress in our students' learning.

There were rich actions that promoted significant learning, such as interactive dictation of contextualized words reflecting on the norms and rules of the Portuguese language, based on the orthographic need of the class to understand regular words, they developed spelling games stimulating the learning of irregular words, such words need to be learned in a different way, as there are no rules for writing them. These activities were also reinforced through the use of educational games.

At the end of these activities, we observed the active participation of all the students, as well as their satisfaction, given that they sought to learn and helped those who showed difficulties during the procedural evaluations, and also verified the progress linked to the curricular competencies. Based on their reflections on issues related to literacy, the teachers understood that in addition to their own mediation, students need to understand how sounds and letters work. They therefore developed activities and used games to consolidate phonological awareness.

Our teachers worked with various textual genres that circulate in society (news, short stories, songs, poems, letters, recipes, advertisements, informative texts, among others, exploring various activities such as crossword puzzles, riddles, word searches, letter scrambles, etc.). They read short stories, exploring prediction and interpretation, stimulating visual and auditory perception, working on oral retelling, as well as exploring comprehension through drawings, dramatizations, sentence formation and word production, awakening new discoveries. Those students who showed autonomy and confidence were encouraged to produce texts in a variety of contexts. The teachers also explored incomplete productions, as well as organizing the texts that had been explored.

The actions planned for teaching were intended to boost the development of executive functions, with the aim of awakening in students their ability to identify and analyze errors, check for discrepancies and observe the absence of logic, making them able to correct their own lapses in various academic subjects (cf. COSENZA; GUERRA, 2011).

Neuroscience has developed its studies in order to understand brain activity and cognition processes, having observed that human learning does not occur from a simple accumulation of perceptual data, but rather from the linking and construction of information arising from perceptions in the brain. The subject, incessantly searching for answers to their conceptions, thoughts and actions, has their neural processes in continuous reorganization and their connective patterns modified at every moment, through processes of enrichment or weakening of synapses (cf. LENT, 2001).

In today's education, each game has its own particularity and capacity to develop the subject, because the differentiated view of play proves the importance of this act. This focus on the actions of play plays an important role in promoting learning and helping to intervene constructively in this process. When children play jigsaw puzzles, for example, they develop visual and perceptual discrimination, and when they play with box puppets, they work on their oral language, manual coordination and learn to locate themselves and dramatize. These are just two games that stand out as examples of the capacity that play has for learning, because when children play, they reveal their mental structures, feelings and thoughts, in other words, their levels of cognitive, affective and social maturity stand out.

The use of toys, games and teaching materials has become an indispensable tool in pedagogical practice because they address the basic demands of the student, starting from what the student already knows and moving on to further learning. When children play, they learn. This is due to the spontaneity of their actions and the opportunity to show what they know and what they don't know. They are not afraid of making mistakes, because they are playing, so there is the possibility of learning from mistakes.

We had the opportunity to witness the development of some of these activities, while others we observed through the results presented in the learning process and the exchange of experiences. These trainings have been satisfactory because their contribution offers theoretical foundations and methodological strategies that enable our students to learn in a meaningful way, contributing to quality education. This can be seen in the change of strategies in the pedagogical practice of our educators, as well as in the application of projects and interdisciplinary didactic sequences with the different curricular components, guaranteeing the right to learn. Educators are understanding the importance of getting students to think about the subject under study, developing activities that will activate various brain connections, relating points that can contribute to long-term memory, knowing that curricular competences can be worked on in various ways and must be explored in different ways, over and over again, so that the process of assimilation, accommodation and equilibration can occur. An example of this understanding was the project run by the Regional Educational Centre of Quixadà, which used the children's song "Dona Aranha" to develop a didactic sequence and contextualized it in various activities, deepening knowledge of the skills being worked on, systematizing and exploring new concepts, as well as successful lessons that left a pleasant impression on its students, as observed in their reports during classroom visits. The following is an example of a meaningful lesson developed by a multi-subject teacher from the Vàrzea da Onça Regional School in the municipality of Quixadà, who has been taking part in PNAIC training since 2013. She worked on interpreting and constructing information in tables and graphs, leading students to realize that this skill could be applied to any day-to-day situation they might encounter with their classmates. The teacher used various materials and toys available at the school. She encouraged the students to collect data, verify this information through organizing activities and understand the data through interviews.

The following is a small survey based on data from this school. During snack time, the teacher proposed a debate about this moment, asking a series of quick questions, presented her questions and then began the interview. As the number of students was small and they were from different grades, the first graders were asked to interview the second graders and vice versa. Once the interview was over, they formulated a table about their favourite snack and a vote was proposed to organize the data needed to construct the graph, after which they were asked about the information they had gathered. The graph was drawn up in the classroom together with the students who collaborated step by step, putting the data and information obtained into the table.

Below are the tables:

SCHOOL MEALS	NUMBER OF STUDENTS
SOPA	04
PORRIDGE WITH DUMPLINGS	02
CHOCOLATE MILK WITH COOKIE	03
RICE WITH CHICKEN	05
JUICE WITH MEAT LOAF	06

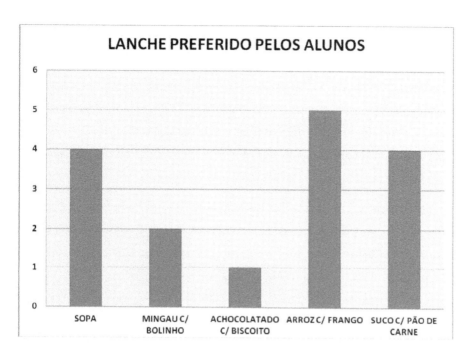

Based on this case study, we can see that the PNAIC training courses are being productive, with various debates taking place, and at the last meeting we commented that the school is, above all, a place where people come together to teach and learn. Based on the studies and research we have been carrying out during the training sessions, we understand that we need a teaching methodology that creates the conditions for students to advance in their learning process, guaranteeing their right to learn, and to learn with quality. This meeting was attended by the PAIC/PNAIC coordinator for the municipality of Quixadà, Rosangela de Almeida Rocha, who said: *"I am happy to see in the eyes of our teachers a thirst for learning, being willing to resignify certain concepts, and this vision was confirmed during visits to the Regional Education Offices to change teaching practices."* This report has taken place on a number of high-profile occasions, such as state seminars, where the municipality was featured in projects selected from successful experiences, both from our actions as study guides and from teachers.

4 CONCLUSION

Based on the research and development of the project, it can be seen that thinking about "quality education" makes it necessary to understand how the learning process takes place in the brain and the relevance of this knowledge on the part of educators, since the purpose of education is only achieved if there is learning, knowing that this process takes place in all social contexts. However, it is in the school institution that academic knowledge is developed, with the teacher mediating this process.

Based on neuroscience, it is known that learning only takes place because the central nervous system has the necessary plasticity to transform itself, reorganize itself in the face of stimuli and adapt. Therefore, we must understand the concept of studying, which is nothing more than a learned behavior, because it is not just about understanding information, but, above all, knowing how to organize it. In this way, teachers can take innovative action, enabling students to develop their own study skills, thus facilitating the acquisition of new knowledge.

In the light of the knowledge of neuroscience, teachers come to realize the importance of practicing emotional intelligence, proposing meaningful pedagogical interventions. It is essential for teachers to be aware of brain structures as interfaces for learning and that this is always a field to be explored. Charming teachers turn information into knowledge and knowledge into experience. It is known that experience is privileged in the fields of memory, capable of transforming personality. That's why it's essential to involve the information they give out in life experience.

Neuroscience alone does not introduce new educational methodologies. It provides important and concrete reasons why some approaches are more effective than others. Exploring the foundations of learning from neuroscience can make a satisfactory contribution to answering some questions, such as: ensuring the success of a curriculum that is compatible with brain development; transforming the knowledge obtained into research and effective instructional methods with real scenarios; improving instruction in subjects; the effect of new technologies on school performance. The educator is the professional who can have the greatest impact on the current education system and from whom much is expected.

According to neuroscience, memory and learning are different phases of the same progressive and continuous mechanism. If there is no memory, learning is unlikely and if there is no learning, there is no memory. Learning, memory and emotion are linked when they are stimulated by the procedures for acquiring knowledge. The challenge for education is not just to know how to teach or how to assess, but to present knowledge in a format that the brain learns best. In learning, which is a social function, students need opportunities to make typical arguments in a calm environment that encourages them to express their feelings and ideas. Every day in the classroom we see a lack of attention on the part of some students, a lack of understanding and poor assimilation, and this has caused many teachers anguish because they don't know how to alleviate these problems. This fact is observed by many educators who often blame the child or adolescent for not having learned, labeling them as uninterested, among other terms. However, some education professionals are unaware of scientific topics that can contribute to understanding these behaviors, because the academic training process did not include greater knowledge in this regard.

The educator plays a fundamental role in the formation of the subject; for this reason, continuous updating and critical reflection on their practice and pedagogical proposal is essential. A number of recent scientific discoveries about the human mind confront some traditional teaching practices that have been applied for years and do not take into account the evolution of the brain and its organization. It is known that the development of learning takes place differently in each individual, so we must try to understand each person's way of learning, analyzing their process, in order to create pedagogical strategies that allow each person to learn in a satisfactory and increasingly efficient way.

In the course of the research, it was noted that there is a need for more investment in linking knowledge of education with neuroscience, since teachers also need to know and understand the influence of biological and social aspects that have an impact on their students' learning, It is at this point that participatory management makes all the difference, because this management strives to organize institutions and mobilize professionals to improve the quality of teaching, seeking to meet the current demands of the contemporary world, to train reflective and critical subjects with the world around them.

REFERENCES

ALVAREZ. A.; LEMOS, I. C. **Os neurobiomecanismos do aprender:** a aplicação de con- ceitos no dia-a-dia escolar e terapêutèutico. Revista de Psicopedagogia, Sâo Paulo, v. 23, n. 71/2006.

ASSMANH, Hugo. **Reenchanting education:** towards a learning society. Petrópolis: Vozes, 2001.

Barros, R. B. (2001). **Grupo:** estratégia na formaçâo. In: J. Brito, M. E. Barros, M. Y. Neves & M. Athayde (Orgs.), *Trabalhar na escola: só inventando o prazer*. Rio de Janeiro: Ed. IPUB.

Borrasca BJ. **Conocimiento profesional y buenas pràcticas en la educacion superior:** genesis y influencias mutuas entre los saberes disciplinares y pedagógicos Del profesorado universitario [doctoral thesis]. Barcelona: Universitat de Barcelona; 2008.

BLANK, M.; ROSE, S. A. & BERLIN, L. J. (1978).The language of learning: the pre-school years. New York, Grune and Stratton.

CARVALHO, F. A. H. **Neuroscience and education:** a necessary articulation in teaching action. In: Trabalho, Educaçâo e Saùde, Rio de Janeiro, v. 8 n. 3, p. 537-550, nov. 2010/feb. 2011.

CORDIOLLI, μ. Brasilia : Câmara dos Deputados, Ediçoes Câmara, 2011.106 p. - (Série açao parlamentar ; n. 436). PFROMM, S. N. *Psicologia da aprendizagem e do ensino*. Sâo Paulo: EPU, 1987.

COSENZA, R. M; GUERRA, L. B. *Neurociência e Educaçâo*. Porto Alegre: Artmed, 2011.

De-NARDIN, M. H.; SORDI, R. O. **A study on the forms of attention in the classroom and their implications for learning.** Psychol. Soc. vol.19 no.1 Porto Alegre Jan./Apr. 2007-   Research conducted -02/03/2014   .   http://dx.doi.org/10.1590/S0102-71822007000100014

Facci, M. G. D. (2004). *Valuing or emptying the work of the teacher? A critical-comparative study of the theory of the reflective teacher, Constructivism and Vygotskian psychology*. Campinas: Autores Associados.

FREIRE, P. *Pedagogia da Autonomia: saberes necessàrios à pràtica educativa*. 37ª ed. Rio de Janeiro: Paz e Terra, 2008.

FENKER, D.; SCHUTZE, H. (2008). Learning By Surprise. *Scientific American*. Published on 17/12/2008. Research carried out on 01/03/2014.

http://www.scientificamerican.com/article/learning-by-surprise/

FONSECA, V. D. **Cogniçao, neuropsicologia e aprendizagem:** abordagem neuropsicologia e psicopedagógica. 2.ed. Petrópolis, Rio de Janeiro: Vozes, 2008.

GADOTTI, M. **Boniteza de um sonho:** *ensinar-e-aprender com sentido.* Sao Paulo: Paulo Freire Institute, 2008.

GARDNER, H. **Structures of the mind** - The theory of multiple intelligences. Porto Alegre: Artmed, 1994.

Gonçalves, M. A. **Sentir, pensar, agir:** *corporeidade e educaçao.* 11ª ed. Campinas/SP: Papirus, 2010.

HARDIMAN, M.; DENCKLA, M. B. (2009). *The Science of Education*: Informing Teaching and Learning through the Brain . Research conducted - 24/02/2014 Sciences. http://www.dana.org/news/cerebrum/detail.aspx?id=23738 18.

http://portal.mec.gov.br/index.php?Itemid=86&id=231&option=com content&view=article Searched on 08/08/2014

http://www.idadecerta.seduc.ce.gov.br/index.php/component/content/article/3-slider- main/433-paic-reduces-child-literacy-review- Survey Conducted - 20/07/2014.

http://www.paic.seduc.ce.gov.br/Pesquisa Held - 20/07/2014

valuehttp://www.spaece.caedufjf.net/ Survey Conducted - 20/07/2014

http://www.si3.ufc.br/sigaa/public/curso/curriculo.jsf;jsessionid=E6546E4B8981AD11C01C5 CA112E3A0D3.node147 Searched on 08/08/2014.

http://www.uece.br/uece/index.php/graduacao/presenciais - searched on 30/07/2014. http://www.uvanet.br/ - searched on 30/07/2014.

KANDEL,E.R.; SCHWARTZ, J. H.; JESSEL, T. M. **Fundamentals of Neuroscience and Behavior.** Trad. By Charles A. Esbérard Mira de C. Engelhardt. Revised by Charles A. Esbérard.1st ed. Rio de Janeiro: Drewtice - Hall do Brasil, 1997.

KEOUGH, B. K. **Children's temperament and teachers' decisions**. In R. Porter & G. M. Collins (eds.), Temperamental differences in infants and Young children. London, Pitman, 1982.

LeDOUX, J. *The emotional brain.* Rio de Janeiro: Objetiva, 2001.

LENT, Robert. **One hundred billion neurons:** fundamental concepts of neuroscience. Sao Paulo: Atheneu, 2001.

LEPPER, M. R.; SETHI, S.; DIALDIN, D.; DRAKE, M. **Intrinsic and extrinsic motivation:** a developmental perspective. In LUTHAR, S. S.; BURACK, J. A.; CICCHETTI, D. & WEISZ J. R. (Orgs.) *Developmental psychopathology - perspectives on adjustment, risk, and disorder* (pp. 23-50).

United States: Cambridge University Press, 1997.

LIBÂNEO, J. C. A **Didàtica e a Aprendizagem do Pensar e do Aprender:** a teoria histórico-cultural da atividade e a contribuição de Vasili Davydov. Revista Brasileira de Educaçâo 2004; 27:5-24.

LUCK, Heloisa. *Gestao Educacional: uma questão paradigmatica.* 3ª ed. Sâo Paulo: Vozes, 1999.

OLIVEIRA, C. E. N.; SALINA, M. E.; ANNUNCIATO, N. F. **Environmental factors that influence CNS plasticity.** *Revista Acta Fisiàtrica,* 2001. 8 (1): 6-13.

PERRENOUD, Philippe. **Ten new skills for teaching.** Porto Alegre: Artes Médicas, 2000.

MACHADO, Â. **Functional Neuroanatomy.** 2. ed. Sâo Paulo: Atheneu, 2004.

MALLOY-DINIZ , L. F. [et al.]. **Neuropsychological assessment** - Porto Alegre: Artmed. 2010. 432p.

MORAES, Maria Cândida; TORRE, **Saturnino de la.** *Sentipensar*: fundamentos e estratégias para reencantar a educaçâo. Petrópolis: Vozes, 2004.

MORALES, R. *Education and neurosciences: a two-way street.* In: **Proceedings of the 28th ANPED Meeting,** Caxambu-MG, 2005.

MORRIS, R.; FILLENZ, M. (eds) (2003). *Neuroscience: The Science of the Brain.* The British Neuroscience Association .The Sherrington Buildings. British Neuroscience Association and the Dana European Alliance for the Brain search conducted on 02/03/2014, on the World Wide Web:

NÓVOA, A. (org). *Teacher training and the teaching profession. Teachers and their training.* Lisbon: Publicaçoes. Dom Quixote, 1997.

NUNES, A. I. B. L; SILVEIRA, R. D. N. **PSYCHOLOGY OF LEARNING:** processes, theories and contexts. Brasilia: Liber livros, 2009.

PANTANO, T; ZORZI, J. L. **NEUROSCIENCE APPLIED TO LEARNING.** 1.ed. Sâo José dos Campos, Sâo Paulo: Pulso, 2009.

PINTRICH P. R.; SCHUNK, D. H. *Motivation in education - theory, research and applications.* New Jersey: Merril Prentice Hall, 2002.

POSNER, Michael I.; RAICHLE, Marcus E. **Images of the mind.** Porto: Porto Editora, 2001.

PROJETO DE LEI DO PLANO NACIONAL DE EDUCAÇÃO (PNE 2011/2020) : projeto em tramaticação no Congresso Nacional / PL no 8.035 / 2010 / organization: Màrcia Abreu e

RELVAS, M. P. **Neurociências e Transtornos** de **Aprendizagem**: as mùltiplas eficiências para educaçâo inclusiva.5.ed - Rio de Janeiro:Wak Ed., 2011. 19

ROTTA, N. T. **Transtornos da Aprendizagem.** Porto Alegre: Artmed, 2006.

SAVIANI, D. *Pedagogia histórico-critica: primeiras aproximçoes.* (8ª ed.). Campinas: Cortez, 2003. Autores Associados.

SIGEL, I. E. & McGILLICUDDY-DELISI, I. **Parents as teachers of their children in the development of oral and written language:** readings in developmental and applied linguistics. Norwood, NJ, Ablex, 1988.

STERNBERG, R. J. & GRIGORENKO, E. L. **Full intelligence: teaching and encouraging student learning and achievement.** Porto Alegre: Artmed, 2003.

TACCA, M. C. V. R. **Teaching and learning:** analyzing processes of meaning in the relationship between teacher and student in structured contexts. Brasilia, 2000. Thesis (PhD) University of Brasilia.

TUNES, E.; TACCA, M. C. V. R.; B ARTHOLO JÙNIOR, R. S. **O professor e o ato de ensinar.** Cad.Pesquisa 2005;126(35): 689 - 698.

WILLINGHAM, D. T. **Why Students Don't Like School:** Answers from Cognitive Science to Make the Classroom More Attractive and Effective, Editora: Penso, 2011.

WOOD, D. *How Children Think and Learn: the social contexts of cognitive development.* São Paulo: Loyola, 2003.

VYGOTSKY, L. S. **The Construction of Thought and Language.** São Paulo: Martins Fontes, 2000.

APPENDICES

QUESTIONNAIRE-OI

01. What role do you play in primary education?

Lecturer

Pedagogical Director

- Other (please specify):_____

02. What is your background?

Pedagogy

Other (please specify):_____

03. How long have you been a graduate?

___ I'm still studying at university

Up to 5 years

-Between 5 and 10 years

04. Do you know about the advances in Neuroscience?

Yes

Some things

ZZ|No

05. Do you think there is a connection between the subjects covered in literacy and neuroscience? Please explain.

Yes, of course.

Yes, rarely

| No, never

06. When designing activities for your students, do you take into account how the brain learns? Why?

Yes, of course.

Yes, rarely

No, never

APPENDIX - B

07. Do you usually use fun activities to reinforce content, taking into account how the brain works? Please explain.

Yes, sometimes.

Yes, rarely

No, never

08. Usually look for it:

Puzzles

Games and magazines

Other (please specify): _____

09. In your opinion, do you consider it essential to have knowledge of how learning takes place in the brain in order to provide a satisfactory response to your information needs in your area of work? Please explain.

Yes

No

I don't know

10. What suggestions do you have for us?

CLASSROOM OBSERVATION
EDUCATIONAL REGION: SCHOOL:_____

SME TECHNICIAN: TEACHER'S NAME:

SUBJECT: YEAR/CLASS:

STUDENTS ENROLLED: DAY'S ATTENDANCE:DATE: _____ / _ /

EDUCATIONAL ASPECT	DETAILS	Yes	No	In part	Not observed	REFERRALS
1. interaction between students and content	- Is the content appropriate to the learning needs of the class?					
	- Are the activities and problems proposed challenging and useful for all students or were they too easy for some and too difficult for others?					
	- Is there a resumption of knowledge worked on in previous lessons as a starting point to facilitate new learning, or do the activities just bring into					

	DETAILS	Yes	No	In part	Not observed	REFERRALS
	play what the class already knows?					
	- Are the resources used appropriate to the content?					
	- How is class time organized? Are there enough periods set aside for students to take notes, ask questions, discuss and solve problems?					
	- Does the teacher select and organize the content in a way that promotes meaningful learning for the students?					
	- Do the students participate in class, actively interacting in the proposed activities?					
2. Interaction between teacher and students	- Does the teacher make the learning objectives of the short and long-term content clear to the class?					
	- Were the proposed activities understood by everyone? Would it be necessary for the teacher to explain again and in a different way? Is the information he gives enough to move the group forward?					
	- Are the interventions made at the right time and do they contain information that helps the students to reflect?					
	- Does the teacher wait for the students to finish their reasoning or does he/she show anxiety about giving the final answers, preventing thinking from evolving?					
	- Are the hypotheses and errors that arise taken into account when developing new problems?					
	- Are individual doubts socialized and used as learning opportunities for the whole class?					
	- Does the teacher keep track of student discipline?					
	- Does the teacher manage the classroom in such a way as to successfully deal with unforeseen issues?					

EDUCATIONAL ASPECT	DETAILS	Yes	No	In part	Not observed	REFERRALS
3. Student interaction with colleagues	- The students feel free to put your hypotheses and opinions?					
	- In pair or group activities there are an exchange of ideas about the content?					
	- In the classroom the students are organized					

	freely or are there pre-established criteria?				
	- There are acts of solidarity in the relationship between each other?				
	- Do the students listen to each other?				
4. The teacher's pedagogical stance	- Does the teacher identify the students' learning difficulties and promote effective interventions?				
	- Is the teacher observing students' daily attendance and taking measures to reduce school dropout?				
	- Does the teacher use targeted techniques/strategies in ongoing training?				
	- Does the teacher use a methodology that involves all the students?				
	- Does the teacher use "homework" as a pedagogical technique to reinforce learning, correcting it collectively in the next class and clarifying students' doubts?				
	- Is there an organized routine in the classroom?				
	- Do the students follow the organized routine?				
5. Use of teaching time	- Does the class start and finish on time, according to the official school timetable?				
	- Is recess/break time used rationally so as not to compromise classroom time?				
	- Does the teacher carry out timed activities in order to make good use of the student's teaching time in the classroom?				
	- Is the annual workload (800 h/a) respected in the classroom?				
	- Does the teacher make rational use (with prior planning) of the student's teaching time with activities outside the classroom?				
6. Environment	- Is the classroom environment comfortable?				
	- Does the classroom have the characteristics of a learning environment?				
	- Is the space airy, well lit?				
	- Is the space clean?				

	- Is the space well maintained?				
	- Are the desks arranged to promote student learning?				
	- Is the space adequate for teaching activities?				
	- Are the walls decorated (posters, ornaments, pictures, etc.)?				
	- Are the walls clean and graffiti-free?				
7. Posture teacher's body	- Does the teacher move around the classroom frequently?				
	- Does the teacher adopt a relaxed and appropriate posture?				
	- Does the teacher stand in a position where all the students can see him?				
	- Do you wear appropriate clothing?				
EDUCATIONAL ASPECT	DETAILS	Yes	No	In part	Not observed	REFERRALS
8. Lesson preparation and planning	- Is the teacher's content coherent with the lesson plan?				
	- Do the students' progress and difficulties perceived by the teacher promote the "re-planning" of didactic-pedagogical actions?				
	- Is the lesson plan developed/used by the teacher in the classroom?				
	- Is the planning (monthly/weekly) carried out in line with the annual plan drawn up at the beginning of the school year? CLASS DIARY/PLAN				
9. Material used	- Does the teacher use different materials?				
	- Is the amount of material used sufficient for teaching practice?				
	- Is the equipment/materials of the Multimedia Center and the School Computer Laboratory - LEI used in the application of the teacher's didactic techniques?				
10. Exposition of the content	- When explaining the content, does the teacher use clear, understandable language (appropriate to the level of the students)?				
	- Do the students concentrate during the lectures?				

	- Does the teacher have a good grasp of the content?				
	- Use your voice properly.				
	- Do you use moderate gestures that match your speech?				
11. Conflict management	- Are there conflicts in the classroom between students?				
	- Are existing conflicts managed in the classroom itself?				
	- Does the teacher mediate to ease conflict situations?				
	- Are there severe punishments for students in the classroom?				
	- Does the teacher take educational measures to correct any atypical situations in the classroom routine?				

OTHER OBSERVATIONS MADE:

FEEDBACK TO THE TEACHER:

SIGNATURES:

ANNEXES

ANNEX A - PHOTOS

I want morebooks!

Buy your books fast and straightforward online - at one of world's fastest growing online book stores! Environmentally sound due to Print-on-Demand technologies.

Buy your books online at
www.morebooks.shop

Kaufen Sie Ihre Bücher schnell und unkompliziert online – auf einer der am schnellsten wachsenden Buchhandelsplattformen weltweit! Dank Print-On-Demand umwelt- und ressourcenschonend produziert.

Bücher schneller online kaufen
www.morebooks.shop

 info@omniscriptum.com
www.omniscriptum.com

Milton Keynes UK
Ingram Content Group UK Ltd.
UKHW032318221024
449917UK00001B/180